A Changing Planet

by John Stafford
illustrations by Scott A. Scheidly

Harcourt Brace & Company

Orlando   Atlanta   Austin   Boston   San Francisco   Chicago   Dallas   New York   Toronto   London

Carl Star lived far, far
away on Snarf. Snarf was a
charming planet.

Carl Star was charming, too.
Carl Star liked art and
played the harp.

Carl Star had a farm in a
marsh on Snarf. His farm
had a charming garden in
the yard.

4

Carl Star had a charming
Snarf car—a sharp-looking
Snarf car.

One dark night, a rocket
sparked down to the marsh
on Snarf. It parked on Carl
Star's farm.

Out jumped Bart Darling
from Gark. "Don't harm me!"
Bart said.

Carl Star said, "I won't harm you, Bart Darling. How can I help you?"

"I must go back to Gark,"
said Bart Darling.
"My Snarf car can get you
back to Gark," said Carl Star.

"A car?" asked Bart Darling.
"A car can't fly to Gark!
No car can go that far!"

"My Snarf car will fly you to
Gark and fly back to Snarf!"
said Carl Star.
Bart Darling marched up
to the car.

"What a charming planet!"
said Bart Darling.